Save Our Earth

By Sharon Stewart

CELEBRATION PRESS
Pearson Learning Group

The following people from **Pearson Learning Group**
have contributed to the development of this product:

Joan Mazzeo, Jennifer Visco **Design** | **Editorial** Betsy Niles, Donna Garzinsky
Christine Fleming **Marketing** | **Publishing Operations** Jennifer Van Der Heide
Production Laura Benford-Sullivan
Content Area Consultant Amy Keller

The following people from **DK** have
contributed to the development of this product:

Art Director Rachael Foster

Sian Williams, Georgina Ackroyd **Design** | **Managing Editor** Scarlett O'Hara
Frances Vargo **Picture Research** | **Editorial** Nada Jolic
Richard Czapnik, Andy Smith **Cover Design** | **Production** Rosalind Holmes
Roger Few **Consultant** | **DTP** David McDonald

Dorling Kindersley would like to thank: Peter Bull for original artwork and Johnny Pau for additional cover design work.

Picture Credits: Corbis: Christies Images 5t; Terry W. Eggers 3r; Najlah Feanny 7t; Jon Feingersh 29b; Lowell Georgia 6b; Don Hammond 1; Paul Hardy 8b; James Leynse 6cr; Will and Deni MacIntyre 10l; Kevin R. Morris 21t; Francesc Muntada 18; Steve Strickland 16t. Ecoscene: Nick Hawkes 16bl; Kevin King 24tl; Lorenzo Lees 25tr; John Wilkinson 17.Getty Images: AFP 7br; Jim Corwin 22bl; Art Wolfe 4l; Joseph Van Os 9t. Nature Picture Library: Stephen David Miller 15tr. Newspix Archive/Nationwide News: 19, 30. N.H.P.A.: Martin Harvey 26bcl. NOAA: Mary Hollinger 28bl. Oxford Scientific Films: Michael Fogden 27br. Pa Photos: EPA 14t. Science Photo Library: Hank Morgan 20br; Ron Sanford 18br;Erika Stone 23br. Still Pictures: Mark Edwards 12r, 14bl; Fritz Polking 26l; Jorgen Schytte 11b; David Woodfall 15br. UN/DPI Photo: 29crb. Jacket: Alamy Images: Bill Bachmann front bl. Corbis: Jon Feingersh back. Getty Images: David Woodfall front t.

All other images: ▨ Dorling Kindersley © 2005. For further information see www.dkimages.com

Special thanks: PhysicsWeb (http://physicsweb.org) for the World Energy Use data on page 8.

ISBN: 0-7652-5229-5

Color reproduction by Colourscan, Singapore
Printed in the United States of America
  6 7 8 9 10   08 07

1-800-321-3106
www.pearsonlearning.com

Contents

endangered golden mantella frog

Natural Resources Affect Our Lives

Try to imagine what life would be like if all our natural resources were gone. You could not turn on a light because there would be no **energy** for electricity. You could not have a glass of water to drink because there would be no clean water.

A natural resource is something from nature that people use to live. Soil, air, water, oil, and coal are natural resources. There are two kinds of natural resources. Renewable resources can replace themselves over time. Animals, plants, soil, water, and wind are examples. Nonrenewable resources cannot be replaced once they are used up. These include coal, oil, and natural gas. We cannot live without natural resources. Therefore, we need to begin to protect them.

The paper for this book came from a tree.

This painting shows the Industrial Revolution in France in the 1800s.

Industry Changed the World

In the late 1700s and 1800s, Europe and North America went through a period called the Industrial Revolution. Machines were invented that could make products very quickly. Soon, factories were built in cities. The factories and machines burned **fossil fuels**, such as coal and oil. The cities grew larger as people moved there to work in the factories.

More and more resources were being used, but no one thought about the effects on the environment. Supplies seemed unlimited, so people thought they would never run out of resources.

Amazing Fact
. . . .
Air **pollution** first became a problem during the 1700s!

Natural Resources Are in Danger

Many nations throughout the world now have factories and industries. These nations are called industrialized nations. Their industries use a large amount of the world's resources. People need natural resources for food, shelter, and clothing. Unfortunately, we are using up all our resources. Renewable resources are being used faster than they can replace themselves.

World Energy Use 1860–1998
Since the Industrial Revolution, people and businesses have used more and more energy.

This rig is drilling for oil, a resource that we must use wisely.

This oil spill caused much damage to the environment in the Gulf of Mexico.

Using up resources is not the only problem. We don't always use our resources wisely. For example, we waste water when we leave the faucet running. We waste the energy from coal or oil when we leave the lights on.

Another problem is the harm done to the environment. One example is pollution. The need for more oil has led to more oil spills as oil is transported mostly by sea. Oil spills damage the ocean **ecosystem**. They kill thousands of animals and plants and pollute the water and land.

A bird covered in oil is rescued from an oil spill in Alaska.

The Importance of Energy

People will always need energy. We need it to heat or cool our homes. Power plants burn coal and oil to make electricity. Electricity provides the energy to power a refrigerator or an air conditioner.

Another reason people need energy is for transportation. Oil is used to make gasoline. Gasoline provides the energy that many cars and trucks need to run.

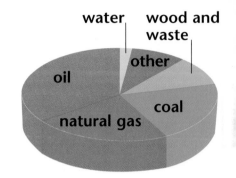

World Energy Use 2000
The world uses mostly fossil fuels to produce energy.

Oil and coal are not renewable resources. We must find new energy sources before our fossil fuels run out. We must also work harder at using less energy. That will make our resources last longer. It will also help to save and protect the environment.

Oil refineries produce oil for the world. They also produce pollution.

Global warming can cause glaciers to melt and form icebergs.

Why Global Warming Is a Problem

Burning fossil fuels harms the environment. This is because of the atmosphere's **greenhouse effect**. Certain gases are naturally trapped in Earth's atmosphere. These gases let in the Sun's energy but trap its heat. When gases from burned fossil fuels get into the atmosphere, more heat is trapped. This changes the climate around the world, which is known as **global warming**.

Changes in climate are dangerous because all living creatures and their **habitats** are affected. Crops may not grow, putting our food supply at risk. The ice caps at the North and South Poles may continue to melt. The sea level will rise, causing flooding and beach erosion. It will also hurt plants and animals near the coast.

The Greenhouse Effect

Gases trap heat in Earth's atmosphere the same way that glass traps heat in a greenhouse. This makes Earth just warm enough for people, animals, and plants to live.

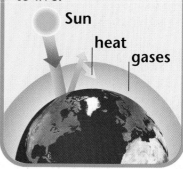

Sun

heat

gases

Air Pollution and Acid Rain

The use of fossil fuels also causes air pollution and **acid rain**. Air pollution can irritate the eyes, nose, and throat. It can also make allergies and asthma worse. Some scientists believe air pollution may cause lung cancer.

healthy yew branch

Gases from burned fossil fuels can combine with rainwater and oxygen to form acid rain. Acid rain is dangerous because it damages or kills plants and trees. It injures the plants' leaves and roots.

dying yew branch

This branch is dying from the effects of acid rain.

Acid rain also pollutes lakes and rivers. This harms some kinds of fish, frogs, and toads. If people eat fish affected by acid rain, they could become sick, too.

Creating Acid Rain

Burning fossil fuels releases polluting gases into the atmosphere. The gases combine with rainwater. The rain becomes a kind of acid. When it falls, acid rain harms animals and plants.

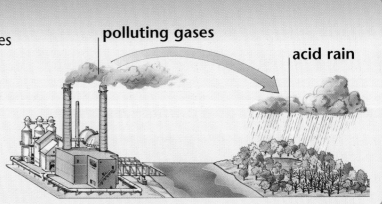

polluting gases

acid rain

Other Energy Sources

There are other sources of energy. These resources include the wind and the Sun. Modern windmills and solar panels provide renewable, inexpensive, and clean energy.

Amazing Fact

. . . .

Wind power was first used to provide electricity in Denmark in the 1890s!

Energy and You

We use natural resources each time we turn on the lights, water, or heat. We can help save our resources by saving energy. Try these energy-saving tips at home:

. . . .

▶ Turn off lights, televisions, and computers when they are not in use.

▶ Ask if your home can be kept warmer in summer and cooler in winter if you use air conditioning and heating.

▶ Ask if fluorescent bulbs can be used. They use less energy than regular light bulbs.

By 2008, people on the island of Samsoe, Denmark, will obtain 100 percent of their energy from renewable resources, such as wind from this wind farm.

We Need Water to Live

Clean water is one of the most important natural resources on Earth. No living creatures can survive without it. Plants would wither and animals would become sick. People, too, need to drink water to stay healthy. We also need water for cooking and washing.

Water is also needed by farmers and industries. Crops must be **irrigated** at the right time in order to grow and produce food. Industries need water to make, clean, or transport their goods. Without water, there would be no food, and industries would fail.

Amazing Fact

· · · · · · · · · · · · ·

You can live for only 3–4 days without water.

These girls in Burkina Faso, West Africa, rely on water from a pump for survival.

Fresh water is only a small amount of the water on the Earth.

Some people might think that water is everywhere. Certainly, more than 70 percent of the Earth is covered with water. Yet most of that water is salty. People and animals can't drink salty water because it makes us sick. It can't be used to water crops either. Only 3 percent of the Earth's water is **fresh water**. Fresh water is what we all need to survive. So, we must keep the water clean and use it wisely.

You Can't Sip the Sea!

This plant makes fresh water from seawater. Scientists use a process called desalinization (dee-sal-ihn-uh-ZAY-shuhn) to remove the salt. Right now, this process is expensive and uses a lot of energy. However, it may be easier and cheaper in the future.

Desalinization plant in Nevada, United States

This flood in the region of Saxony in 2002 was the worst flood in Germany's history.

These girls walk on a dried river bed to get water during a drought in India.

Global Warming and Water

Earth's fresh water supply can be harmed by global warming. Some areas could get more rain than usual. This might cause flooding or damage crops. Other areas could get less rain. Farmland might become too dry to grow crops. Small rivers and ponds could dry up forever.

Global warming might make the oceans warmer. This would be harmful to fish and plants that need cool water. These creatures would need to find cooler habitats or they might die out. Animals that eat these fish would not have food and might have to move or die out, too. The fishing industry would fail without fish.

Polluted Water

Water can become polluted very easily. Energy sources like coal and oil can affect our water in serious ways. Factories often produce large amounts of waste that seeps into the water.

People, cars, and farms contribute to this problem as well. Water from a sprinkler or a garden hose can wash **pesticides**, fertilizers, and car fluids into storm drains. Many storm drains empty into local rivers, streams, lakes, and oceans. The contaminated water then pollutes the rivers and lakes. If the pollution is bad enough, it kills the animals and plants that live there.

These fish died from pollution in Lake Trafford, Florida, United States.

Some storm drains may empty into the ocean. Polluted water in a storm drain will pollute the ocean.

This airplane is spraying pesticides to protect crops. This can result in farm runoff.

Farm runoff caused this algae bloom in Suffolk, England.

Water pollution can also come from farms. Animal waste and pesticides can wash into nearby rivers, streams, and wells. This is called farm runoff. As a result, unhealthy bacteria and harmful chemicals enter the water supply.

To protect the water, we need to be careful. For example, we can be careful about the chemicals we use on our lawns and how we wash our cars. It's also important that farms and factories find ways to avoid polluting the water supply. Plus, we must begin to use fresh water wisely so that it's not wasted. Everyone needs to work together to save our precious water.

Water and You

Everyone can learn how to be wise with water. By protecting water and using less of it, you can help the entire Earth. Here are some water-saving tips:

▶ Never throw waste into an ocean, river, lake, or street drain.

▶ Turn off the faucet while you brush your teeth.

▶ Try a quick shower instead of a bath. That could save up to 100 gallons of water a week.

▶ Tell adults about leaky faucets so they can be fixed.

▶ Use collected rainwater for house and garden plants.

▶ Become involved in a river, stream, or lake cleanup.

Scouts help clean the River Almond in Scotland, United Kingdom.

Amazing Fact

We use more than 50 gallons of water per person every day!

Garbage Causes Big Problems

Even if it is buried in landfills, garbage can still cause big problems.

Household waste is all the garbage we throw away, and we need to produce less of it. Everything we get rid of goes somewhere, so our garbage affects something else in the environment.

Garbage can also be dangerous to people's health. It clutters up the land because much of it, such as disposable diapers, plastic, and glass, will not rot away. Some kinds of garbage, such as plastic, can be dangerous to wildlife. Sea turtles may eat plastic bags that float in the water. Pelicans and sea otters can get tangled up in discarded fishing line.

This sea lion was rescued from a fishing net which had been carelessly thrown out.

When you put out the garbage, where does it go? Some of it may be buried in landfills. These are giant pits where the garbage is dumped and then covered up. The average person in the United States produces about four pounds of garbage a day. It's no surprise that many landfills are full. Some communities have so much garbage that they have to send it to other places.

Space is not the only problem. Some garbage, such as paint or cleaners, contains harmful chemicals. If these chemicals leak into the soil around a landfill, they may get into the local water supply and pollute it.

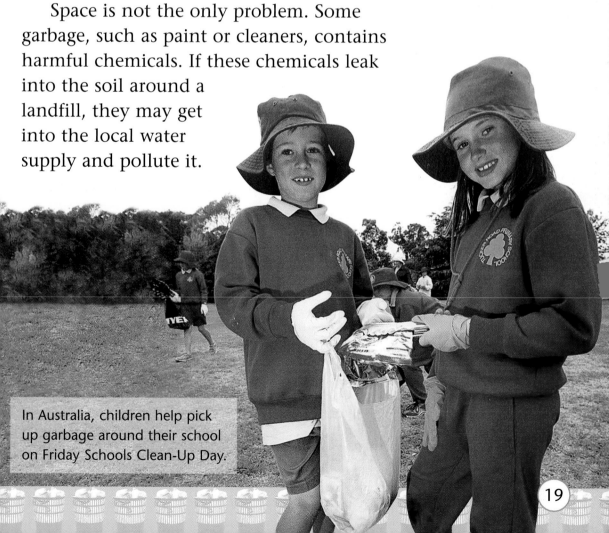

In Australia, children help pick up garbage around their school on Friday Schools Clean-Up Day.

Parts of a Landfill

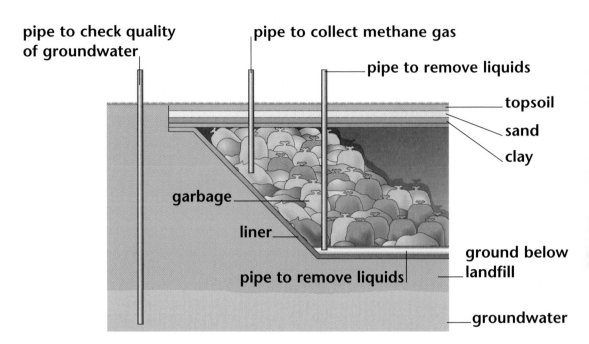

pipe to check quality of groundwater

pipe to collect methane gas

pipe to remove liquids

topsoil

sand

clay

garbage

liner

ground below landfill

pipe to remove liquids

groundwater

Garbage also pollutes the air. That's not just because it smells bad! As garbage rots, it produces a dangerous gas called methane. Methane is one of the gases that contribute to the greenhouse effect, so methane contributes to global warming. Burning garbage is not a solution either. The smoke from burning garbage can also cause air pollution.

Don't Waste Your Energy

Some communities have found ways to handle landfill problems. This power plant in Puente Hills, California, is one example. It uses methane gas from the landfill to produce electricity. At the same time, it keeps the methane out of the air.

The second-hand items for sale at this place in Canada can be reused.

Three words to remember in the battle against waste are *reduce*, *reuse*, and *recycle*. *Reduce* means using less and saving resources. *Reuse* means finding new uses for some things before throwing them away. You can find out more about the third word, *recycle*, in the next chapter.

It's important that we reduce and reuse resources. If we don't, we may run out of space in landfills. We could also run out of resources to make new products.

Waste and You

No one wants to live in a world of garbage. You can help by learning to be wise about waste. Here are some ideas:

Recycle

▶ Don't throw away newspapers, glass, and plastic. Recycle them.

▶ Don't litter. Throw garbage into containers, not on the ground.

Reuse

▶ Use a reusable fabric lunch bag, utensils that can be washed and used again, recycled paper napkins, and reusable plastic containers for food instead of foil or plastic wrap.

Reduce

▶ Before you get something new, ask yourself whether you really need it.

Be a Recycler

Reduce, *reuse*, and *recycle* are the three R's. *Recycle* means to reuse materials by turning them into new products. Recycling saves our natural resources. It also reduces the amount of garbage going into landfills.

Recycling saves energy, too. It takes less energy to recycle materials than to produce them. Saving energy means we cause less air pollution, acid rain, and global warming.

Together, the three R's are important for everyone to do. If we all reduce, reuse, and recycle, we can help to save the Earth.

These are the three R's of a responsible world citizen:
- reduce
- reuse
- recycle

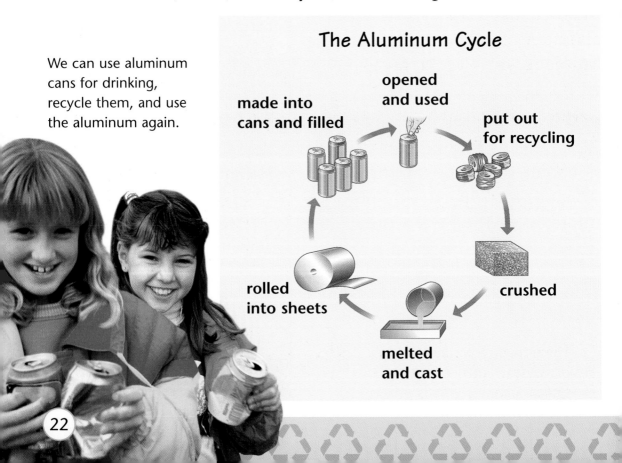

The Aluminum Cycle

We can use aluminum cans for drinking, recycle them, and use the aluminum again.

made into cans and filled

opened and used

put out for recycling

crushed

melted and cast

rolled into sheets

Paper, Plastic, and Glass

Many communities around the world recycle. It's easy to do. Ask an adult to help you. First, find out which materials are recycled where you live. Paper, glass, and plastic are the most common ones. Place the different materials in separate containers. Put them out for collection, or take them to the recycling center.

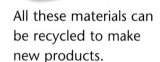

All these materials can be recycled to make new products.

It's also important to buy recycled products or those that can be recycled. This tells manufacturers that people care about recycling. Materials that can be recycled are stamped with a symbol. By buying products that can be recycled, we help to reduce the amount of garbage sent to landfills.

recycling symbols

These children are involved in a recycling program in New York, United States.

Food and Garden Waste

Nature is a great recycler. Tiny bacteria and fungi break down food wastes, grass clippings, and leaves. Worms and insects help, too.

If you have access to an outdoor area, you can make a compost pile. Ask an adult to help you. Put food and garden wastes into the compost container. Don't add meat, oils, or dairy products, though! Turn the mixture over now and then. In six to eight weeks, you may have rich brown compost, or humus. Humus is great for renewing the soil. It helps plants to grow, and it keeps wastes that can be recycled out of our landfills.

You can throw vegetable scraps or moldy vegetables into a compost pile.

This red pepper develops mold on it from the air. In two weeks it goes from red to rotten!

Amazing Fact

. . . .

In a landfill, a banana peel could take six months to a year to break down.

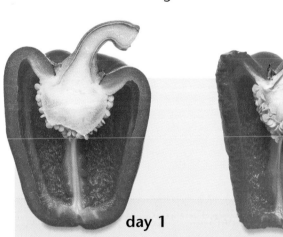

day 1   day 5

Recycling and You

Recycling saves energy and resources. It is a great way to help the Earth. Encourage your family to start a recycling plan. Here are things you can do to get going:

▶ Buy products that can be recycled or that are made of recycled materials.

▶ Separate recyclables by type, such as paper, glass, and plastic.

▶ Help take recyclables to the curb for collection or go to the recycling center.

▶ Carry fruit and vegetable waste to the compost pile. Remember to turn the pile from time to time.

Your community's recycling center might have recycling containers like these in London, England.

day 8

day 10

day 15

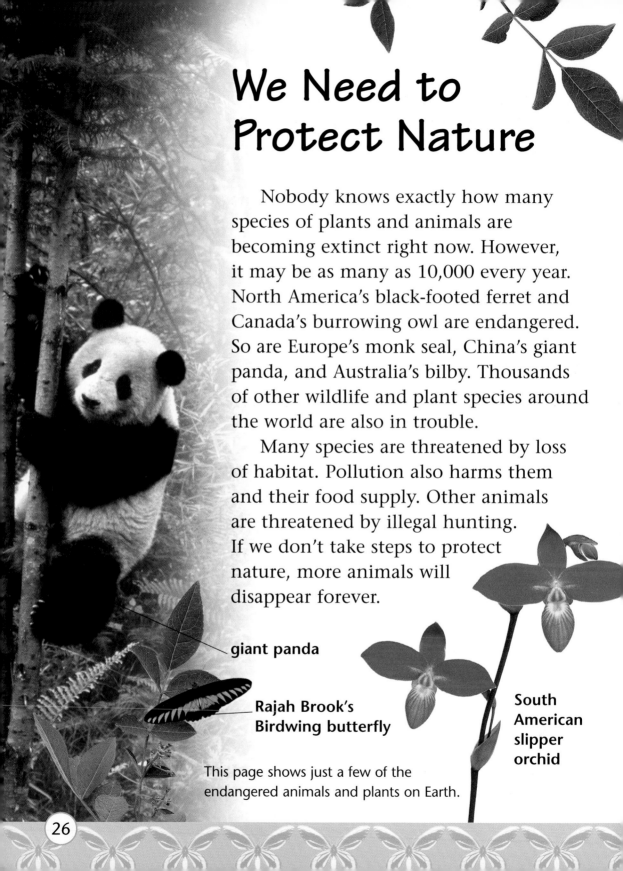

We Need to Protect Nature

Nobody knows exactly how many species of plants and animals are becoming extinct right now. However, it may be as many as 10,000 every year. North America's black-footed ferret and Canada's burrowing owl are endangered. So are Europe's monk seal, China's giant panda, and Australia's bilby. Thousands of other wildlife and plant species around the world are also in trouble.

Many species are threatened by loss of habitat. Pollution also harms them and their food supply. Other animals are threatened by illegal hunting. If we don't take steps to protect nature, more animals will disappear forever.

giant panda

Rajah Brook's Birdwing butterfly

South American slipper orchid

This page shows just a few of the endangered animals and plants on Earth.

Everything in nature is connected. The Earth and all forms of life on it are helped by **biodiversity**. High biodiversity means that many different living things share the same living space. The relationships between the different creatures are important. These relationships form a connection like a web. If one part of the web is broken or dies out, every other part of the web is harmed.

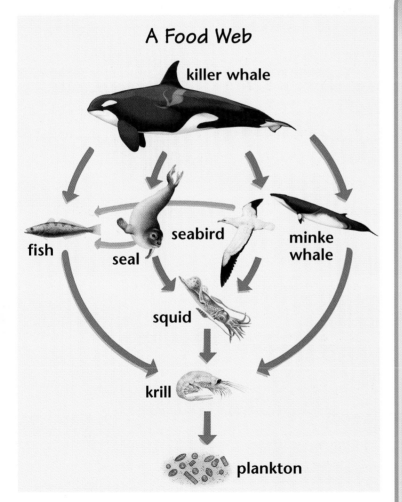

A Food Web

killer whale

fish

seal

seabird

minke whale

squid

krill

plankton

A food web shows how animals and plants depend on each other for food.

The Important Antbird

Losing a species of animal could affect a whole ecosystem. Antbirds live in the rain forest in South America. They eat insects. If the antbirds disappeared, there would be too many insects. The insects would then destroy some of the plants in the rain forest. The plants produce oxygen, which humans need to breathe.

Forests are a good example of ecosystems that support biodiversity. Many different plants and animals find food and shelter in forests. Likewise, plants and animals provide food for the trees.

If a forest is damaged or destroyed, all the animals and plants that live there will be harmed in some way. They might need to find a new forest to live in. If they can't, they and the plants and animals that depend on them might die out.

These children are learning about the ecosystems in this swamp in Maryland, United States.

Amazing Fact

More than 4,500 types of animals and plants in the world are endangered.

Saving the World

People need natural resources to live, therefore, we must use them wisely. Imagine a world where the air is dirty. The trees have all been cut down. The water is polluted. The soil is dry and bare. No one would want a world like that.

Our natural resources are disappearing fast. We have already destroyed half of the world's forests. If we continue using oil so quickly, some scientists say we won't have enough for everyone by 2020. By 2025, 3 billion people may not have clean water.

It sounds serious, doesn't it? It is, but you *can* make a difference. It's never too late to take action. Just get started *now*!

Earth Summit

In 2002, many nations attended a meeting in Johannesburg, South Africa. It was called an Earth Summit. Many children contributed posters about saving and protecting our resources. This poster is called "Destiny Weights." It was drawn by an Armenian girl, named Melanya Hamasyan.

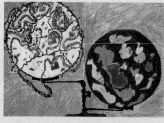

"Destiny Weights" ▲

Plant a tree.
Help save the Earth.

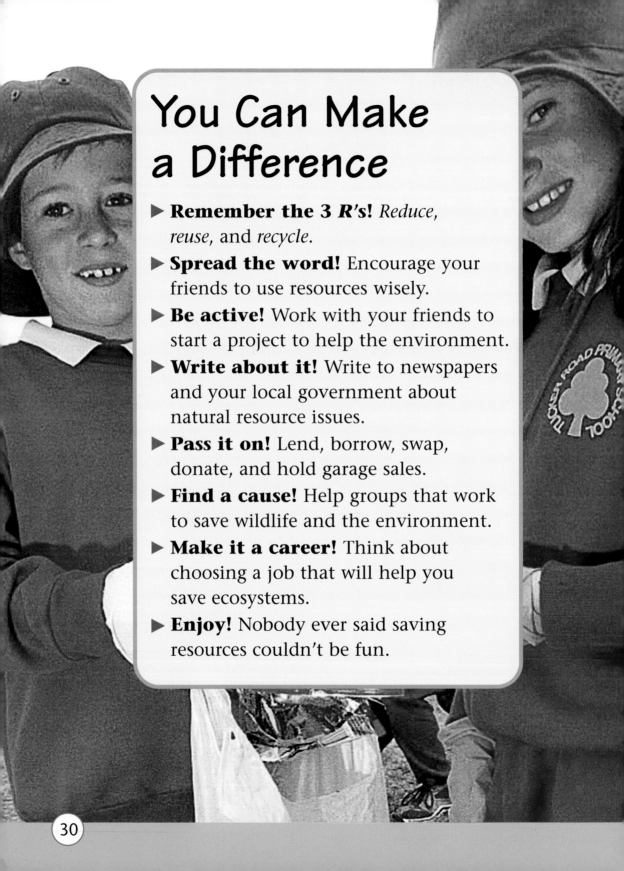

You Can Make a Difference

▶ **Remember the 3 *R*'s!** *Reduce, reuse,* and *recycle.*

▶ **Spread the word!** Encourage your friends to use resources wisely.

▶ **Be active!** Work with your friends to start a project to help the environment.

▶ **Write about it!** Write to newspapers and your local government about natural resource issues.

▶ **Pass it on!** Lend, borrow, swap, donate, and hold garage sales.

▶ **Find a cause!** Help groups that work to save wildlife and the environment.

▶ **Make it a career!** Think about choosing a job that will help you save ecosystems.

▶ **Enjoy!** Nobody ever said saving resources couldn't be fun.

Glossary

acid rain rain that contains acids, which is formed when air pollutants mix with water vapor

biodiversity the variety of living things on Earth or within a region

ecosystem all the living and nonliving things in an environment and how they interact

energy power obtained from natural resources

fossil fuels fuels formed over many years from plant and animal remains

fresh water water that is not salty and can be used for drinking and farming

global warming an increase in the Earth's temperature

greenhouse effect warming of the Earth's atmosphere caused by gases trapping heat from the Sun in the atmosphere

habitats the environments in which plants or animals live

irrigated supplied with water from hoses, pipes, or ditches

pesticides substances that kill or keep away pests or insects

pollution harmful substances that dirty the air, water, or soil

Index